Managing Emotions

*How to Stay Calm When
Facing Stress, Pressure,
or Frustration*

by Melinda Bauer

Table of Contents

Introduction

Emotions are what make us human. They allow us to experience feelings of happiness, sadness, pleasure, pain, excitement, and boredom. In this way, they make us feel alive!

The downside to this, however, is that sometimes negative emotions seem to take the reins and get the best of us. If we're not careful, we inadvertently allow our emotions to rule us instead of the other way around. When this happens, it's difficult to think rationally, and problems usually occur as a result. We tend to do unpleasant things that we often regret later on.

This book is designed to assist you in managing your emotions and controlling your emotional responses to external factors. It will provide specific steps to train yourself how to stay calm during stress and to remain happy regardless of external pressure or frustrating circumstances. By learning how to control your emotions instead of allowing them to control you, you're going to discover a new level of self-resiliency that will transform various other aspects of your life as well, from the foundation up. If this sounds exciting to you, then let's get started!

Chapter 1: Understanding How Emotions Manifest

You hear people say that emotions come from the heart. This is not scientifically true because emotions come from the hypothalamus, the part of the brain that recognizes and responds to stimuli. From a scientific standpoint, therefore, feelings of love and all other emotions emanate from the hypothalamus. Therefore, instead of saying "I love you with all of my heart", it is actually more accurate to say "I love you with all of my hypothalamus."

Physiology of emotions

The brain is the center of the Central Nervous System (CNS). The CNS is responsible for transmitting and receiving nerve impulses from the different portions of the body. There are various receptors in the body that help in the transmission of stimuli so that the body can react.

Common types or receptors

Pain receptors

The pain receptors, also called nociceptors, are present in all parts of the body. These receptors aid in keeping you safe from pain and injury. Through the exposure of the free nerve endings, the body can feel pain when these nociceptors send a signal to the brain. This stimulus is then recognized by the brain (hypothalamus) and the person will feel the pain. This explains why a person cannot feel anything when he is unconscious.

Cold and heat receptors

These are also called thermoreceptors. These receptors are in-charge of allowing you to feel cold or heat. Just like the nociceptors, the brain has to recognize the stimulus before your body can "feel" anything, in this case—cold and heat.

Touch, position, sensation or pressure receptors

These are called mechanoreceptors. You can "feel" touch, pressure sensations, through these receptors within the skin. They feed the stimuli to the brain.

Tactile receptors are involved in the recognition of touch, vibration and pressure sensations. They transmit the exact body location, type of pressure, the size and the type of movement applied on that area. These receptors have a crucial role in the production of emotions.

When a person touches you, your tactile receptors or mechanoreceptors respond. The brain will now recognize the message and you can feel the sensation of touch.

Chemoreceptors

These are receptors that are triggered by water and lipid soluble chemicals. They respond to chemical stimulus that the body is susceptible to.

Baroreceptors

These receptors are responsible for sending nerve impulses to the brain regarding changes in pressure in the different organs of the body.

Proprioceptors

These receptors send nerve impulses about the position of joints, muscles and any muscular activity.

All these receptors play a key role in the emotions that you feel. When a person lovingly caresses your skin, you can feel either a surge of love or indifference. When a person pushes you rudely, the pressure applied to your body will be transmitted to your brain and you feel anger or understanding. The parasympathetic and sympathetic systems work together too, for you to be able to feel these sensations.

Hence, when your skin comes in contact with a hot stove, this stimulus is fed to your brain and you feel the heat as your body's reflexes respond involuntarily to get away from the source of the stimulus—the hot stove. If your right body part is injured, the left portion of your body will respond to get you away from the stove; your left foot takes a step backward. There are other involuntary body responses that happen instantly, such as the body reflexes like knee jerks or eye blinking. The brain's reaction is typically quick and automatic, except when there is brain dysfunction.

You should know that the emotions that you feel are controlled by your brain. Your brain has the power not to acknowledge the stimulus. Hence, when the brain consciously refuses to react to the stimulus, your body won't respond.

Once you are aware that your emotions are controlled by your brain, you can control your emotions by learning how to consciously command your brain.

Chapter 2: Staying Calm in the Face of Stress and Pressure

Staying calm in the face of stress and pressure can be difficult. But with determination and practice, you can do it. Remember the fact that your emotions are controlled by your brain. So, what should you strive to control? Understandably, it would be your brain. Stress, pressure and frustration are normal parts of everybody's daily existence, and you cannot eliminate them totally; you will have to cope with them and learn how to stay calm in spite of outside factors. Learn to master the following simple steps to train yourself to respond with calm and grace under any given circumstances.

Step #1—Identify the source of your stress or pressure

When you know what's stressing or pressuring you, you will know who the enemy is. Know your enemy and you can get rid of it quickly.

Step #2—Desensitize yourself

Once you've identified your stress or pressure triggers, you can take steps to get rid of them. If you cannot eliminate the source of your stress and pressure, then you have to desensitize yourself. Desensitization is recommended especially for stress triggers that you cannot eliminate, those that are outside of your control. This is true for situations where trying to avoid these triggers can only stress you more.

Desensitization is done by exposing yourself constantly to stress triggers. For example, if attending math class triggers stress for you, you have to attend lectures religiously and make a point of being present for all class meetings. Do something profitable in class so you can come to love it more. Study well to receive good grades. If the professor is someone who you find intimidating, look for extra opportunities to speak with him outside class to consult on course topics.

Another example is when you're stressed or pressured because of the noise in your workplace and you are not in a position to stop it. Constantly expose yourself to the noise to get you used to it, arrange to make the noise even louder than it normally is while you are trying to desensitize. Once you are used to it, it will no longer stress or pressure you.

Step #3—Change your perception

Believe that anything that your brain doesn't acknowledge will not affect you. Stress and pressure results when you allow circumstances to disrupt your emotions. View the trigger as a button you can turn on and off, so that when you think about it, you don't feel perturbed, and you can remain calm because you know you can turn it off, any time you want to. Psyche your mind that there's nothing to be afraid of, and that you should remain calm. If any negative thing happens, it's still not the end of the world.

Step #4—Perform breathing exercises

Deep breathing exercises are great for keeping calm in the face of stressful situations, when you may be pressured and frustrated. Here is one breathing exercise to use in stressful situations:

1. Stand with your arms akimbo and your back straight. Your feet must be flat on the floor and at least 1 foot apart.

2. Raise your heels as you stand on your toes.

3. Inhale deeply through your nose and feel the air enter your nostrils, and lungs. Your chest must lift up and your abdomen remain relaxed.

4. Hold your breath for 6 seconds (count up to 6, starting with 1,001 up to 1,006).

5. Exhale forcefully through your mouth, as you lower your heels to their original position. Your chest should now be lowered as your abdomen contracts.

6. Mentally instruct the muscles in your body to relax as you continue to inhale and exhale.

7. Do these steps several times until you feel your muscles have relaxed and your stress is alleviated.

You can also get hold of a few sheets of paper in each hand and crumple them to exercise your fingers. You simply crush the pieces of paper in your fingers, while stretching your arms and doing inhalation and exhalation routines.

Do this every time you feel stress creeping out of its shell. Simple breathing exercises will help a lot in releasing stress, if you perform them correctly and consistently.

Step #5—Visualize yourself staying calm

Visualization is one simple but powerful method in coping with stress and pressure. Stay in a quiet corner and visualize yourself staying calm despite the presence of the triggers. Let's say you're scheduled to speak before a group, and you're stressed because it's your first speaking engagement. Play out a script or story in your head where everything goes perfect. Visualize every step, including details of how you want to stay calm. Your mind movie can look something like this:

1. Imagine yourself sitting at the guest chair, calm and composed. You have a bright smile on your face, and your back is straight, exuding self-confidence.

2. Visualize yourself walking confidently to the podium as the Master of Ceremonies calls your name.

3. Imagine yourself delivering your speech with gusto, with the correct gestures, perfect

diction and tone of voice. (Of course, you have practiced delivering your speech repeatedly beforehand.)

4. Imagine the audience listening to you attentively.

5. Visualize the audience's enthusiastic applause at just the right moments during the speech and maybe a standing ovation after.

6. Visualize yourself walking confidently back to your seat, as the audience continues to applaud.

Step #6—Channel your stress and pressure to any fruitful activity

You may be familiar with the cliché, "Turn your lemons into lemonade." With stress, you can do that too. Stress and pressure can motivate you to prepare better for a presentation or an important performance. A little amount of stress and pressure is good to keep you on your toes. You merely have to know how to manage it.

A specific example is this: you're stressed out because of your upcoming career licensure exams. Instead of giving in to stress and worrying yourself to death, you do something fruitful about it; you exert more effort in studying to manage your stress. When you're fully prepared for the exam because you know you have studied well, your stress level will decrease significantly.

Therefore, whatever you're stressed or pressured about; come up with a creative way to use the stress. Reduce fears and anxieties by doing something about them and you'll definitely reduce your stress and frustration, or you can eliminate them altogether.

Step #7—Psyche yourself constantly

Since the brain is responsible for your emotions, you have to psyche yourself repeatedly so that you can calmly deal with stressful situations. You can look at the mirror every morning and tell yourself that you are able to calmly respond to any stressful event or pressure you may encounter during the day.

You can also do this before going to sleep. Keep psyching yourself until the message reaches your subconscious and becomes integrated with your conscious mind. Your conscious mind will then act out what the subconscious mind believes. The combination of the subconscious and the conscious mind can propel the body into performing actions that may at first seem impossible.

The mind is extremely powerful. The motto: "What your mind can conceive, the body can achieve" is totally true. So, get rid of any pessimistic attitude and believe you can conquer stress, pressure and frustration, and remain calm no matter what.

The most common triggers of stress and pressure are fear and anxiety. People fear what they don't know. It's only natural. Hence, by knowing as much as you can about the unknowns you are facing, you can eliminate or decrease stress and pressure in your life. Learn about what triggers your negative emotions. Know your enemy and you can get rid of them successfully. Believe you can overcome them, and you will!

Chapter 3: The Key to Beating Frustration

Dealing with frustration is frustrating. It takes a gargantuan effort to remain calm in the face of frustration. But it's also a fact of life that you have to face. How can you stay calm when you're frustrated? The steps to overcoming frustrating situations are similar to that of coping with stress and pressure.

Step #1—Identify the specific frustration

What are you frustrated about? It must be properly identified and specified. "I'm frustrated about school" is a broad area. Dig deep to get to the root cause: "I'm frustrated because of my failing grade in algebra," could be "I didn't study and therefore failed in the tests" or "I'm frustrated with the negative results of my case presentation." Identifying your frustration will help you resolve it.

Step #2—Evaluate what caused the occurrence

If you're frustrated about a botched presentation, you have to determine what caused the failure. Write down these causes, and opposite the causes cite possible remedies or solutions. Keep this record, so you can refer to it later should a similar circumstance occur. While you're busy trying to figure what went wrong, you're focusing on what you can do and this will help you keep calm. You're doing something about it and learning from your own mistakes.

Step #3—Accept what happened

Accept whatever happened wholeheartedly. Avoid blaming anyone for your frustrations—especially yourself. Just consider the incident as a learning experience. Acceptance will help you move on and will bring a certain calmness to your spirit and mind.

Step #4—Learn to perform quick relaxation exercises

You can perform exercises to relieve your frustrations. Refer to Chapter 2, Step #4, for the deep breathing exercise. You can do this exercise every time you can spare the time. It doesn't only keep you calm but also promptly relieves frustrations.

Step #5—Meditate

Meditating is one sure way to achieve calmness and tranquility of mind. It also allows you to relax and de-stress. There are various methods such as, yoga, one-step, and mindfulness meditation. The steps to the "Walking Meditation" technique are as follows:

Walking Meditation

1. Choose a safe and secure walking area.

2. Wear comfortable shoes and clothing.

3. Morning walks are preferable, but there is nothing wrong with evening walks either.

4. Start walking, using a normal pace. Relax your body and your mind.

5. Focus on your feet. Observe how your toes curl when you lift your feet to step forward. Notice how your calves become tense and relax again when you complete a step.

6. Keep focusing on your feet and legs as you continue with the exercise.

7. Walk for at least 30 minutes, or go for a full hour for maximum benefits.

Step #6—Listen to music

Listening to your favorite music is one way of venting your frustrations. Music is a language that soothes the heart, and is certainly a good method of taking your focus away from your frustrations.

Step #7—Psyche your mind to always stay calm

As previously mentioned, the mind is a powerful tool capable of controlling emotions, so you have to psyche your mind to deal calmly with your frustrations so they pass. Remind yourself that you are the master of your emotions and you have complete control over them. Hence, if you don't want to feel frustrated, you can do so. This may take a bit of work to master, but with practice, you can acquire the habit of staying calm in the face of frustrations. Remember, mind over body. You can do it!

Step #8—Document your experience

Writing down the details, causes, and feelings of frustration will help clarify the issue. It also lets you evaluate situations objectively and draft ensuing plans of action based on your data. Prepare your plan of action carefully. Your plan must have a timetable and the short and long-term goals must be achievable, feasible and relevant.

Step #9—Stand up anew

Frustrations generally result from failure or from unresolved problems. Never give up. Learn from your frustrations and treat them as stepping stones towards success. Keep standing up after your every fall. There's always the hope of an objective being fulfilled as long as you keep trying. As long as you don't quit you have not yet truly failed; remain persistent and determined. Be patient to pursue the short-term and long-term goals you have set for yourself.

These steps effectively work to keep you calm in the face of frustrations. You can do it. You're the master of your own emotions.

Chapter 4: How to Manage Your Emotions

Staying calm in the face of strong, sometimes confusing, emotions is possible with constant practice. Since emotions are a part of life, you cannot escape them altogether. You have got to train yourself to deal with them calmly and productively. Dealing with emotions is similar to coping with stress—you have to use your brain to manage your emotions. Therefore, it's of primary importance that you maintain your brain's health. Here's what you can do to manage your emotions.

Step #1—Determine if the expression of the emotion is beneficial or destructive

Emotions, per se, are not bad, because they are outlets of a person's thoughts and feelings. Still, there are emotions that are interpreted as negative or positive. Positive emotions commonly include love, happiness and joy, while negative emotions may include hatred, sadness, indifference and misery. These "negative' emotions are good in the sense that they allow you to de-stress and release your angst to prevent the accumulation of pent up emotions which can be dangerous to your health.

Your emotions can be likened to a pressure cooker, wherein heat causes the pressure to build up and if you don't release it slowly, it can burst and injure people around it. You have got to express your negative emotions, but you should release them slowly or appropriately. You must not wallow in negative emotions, because then they will cloud your perspective, and even prevent you from achieving happiness.

Step #2—Express your feelings

Once you have determined that expressing a particular emotion is beneficial and will not hurt anyone, express it openly. Common sense will dictate if expressing your emotions is the right thing to do. Nurturing positive emotions is an excellent way to stay healthy. Laughing and smiling relieves stress and frustrations. It will also exercise your muscles and make you more beautiful. That's why they say the best makeup a woman can wear is her smile.

Step #3—Eliminate extremes

It's important to note that extreme expressions can be destructive. Examples are: expressing your anger without restraint, prolonged self-indulgence in sadness, or wallowing in grief. Moderation is the key to managing your emotions well.

Step #4—Get out and exercise

Exercising can reduce stress and help you stay calm. Make it a habit to exercise daily for 30 minutes to 1 hour, or thrice a week for 1 to 2 hours. This will not only relax your muscles and clear your mind, but it will also boost your metabolism, respiratory functions and cardiovascular system. It will reduce your risk of heart attacks and hypertension. When your brain is clear, you can readily control your emotions.

Step #5—Avoid drugs, alcohol, caffeine and nicotine

Drugs affect the CNS considerably; hence your brain's ability to control your emotions can be affected. Alcohol is a CNS depressant that also tends to remove all your inhibitions, causing people to express emotions wantonly, which can be disastrous. Imagine yourself expressing joy by kissing strangers, or by disrobing before them. You'll surely regret expressing your emotions later. In contrast, caffeine is a CNS stimulant; it can make you bold and hyperactive. Nicotine calms the nerves but only temporarily. It's addictive too, which can endanger your health. Avoid these harmful substances so that you can have a clear mind in managing your emotions.

Step #6—Get enough sleep

Studies have proven that lack of sleep decreases the brain's cognitive abilities and disrupts its function. People who were continuously deprived of sleep later start to display symptoms of mental disorder. Getting sufficient sleep (at least 8 hours a day) will ensure that the brain is functioning properly. When the brain functions efficiently, it can control and manage emotions appropriately.

Step #7—Eat foods for brain health

The primary nutrient needed for the brain is glucose that comes from the metabolism of carbohydrates. This is precisely the reason why people faint when they're hungry (called hypoglycemia or low sugar/glucose levels). The brain is the first organ that is affected in hypoglycemia. So, eat enough carbohydrates (rice, pasta, bread, potato) to ensure there's enough energy for your brain to use. But don't overeat; excess carbohydrates can also be disastrous to your health because of the danger of hyperglycemia (increased sugar or glucose levels). It can also increase your risk of acquiring diabetes mellitus. Diabetes is a condition that can inflict harm to the brain and other internal organs.

Other foods that are known to boost brain function are:

- Nuts and legumes (beans, peas, lentils)

- Whole grains

- Avocado

- Blueberries

- Salmon

- Trout

- Mackerel

- Sardines

- Broccoli

- Dark chocolate

- Tomatoes

- Pumpkin seeds

The brain is a powerful tool that you can utilize to change your life forever; that is if you know how to maximize its potential.

Chapter 5: Specific Relaxation Techniques for Trying Times

Practice use of the following strategies that are proven effective in managing emotions and coping with stress, pressure and frustrations:

A. Progressive Muscular Relaxation (PMR)

This is a relaxation technique that allows the muscles to tighten and relax progressively. This is a good de-stressor because it also calms the nerves and clears the brain. This allows you to think clearly and to control your emotions effectively.

<u>Steps</u>

1. Find a quiet and secure place.

2. Loosen any tight clothing and sit or lie down comfortably.

3. Start by doing breathing exercises as explained in Chapter 2, Step #4.

4. After your breathing has stabilized, proceed to PMR.

5. Start with your toes. Curl and relax them slowly, at least 10 to 15 times or as necessary, to obtain complete relaxation. Mentally instruct your toes to tighten up and relax. Feel how they grow heavy as the muscles relax.

6. Proceed to your soles. Contract and relax them too, until they are completely relaxed.

7. Go up your ankles, legs, thighs, pubic muscles, abdomen, chest, shoulders, arms, neck, and then face. You have to dwell in each of these body parts until they are all completely relaxed. Don't proceed to the next body part until you have done the one before. If you notice the other body parts growing tense again, go back and repeat the procedure one more time.

8. After all your lower body parts are relaxed, proceed to your face, pucker your lips and then relax them, do these 10 to 15 times or as necessary to attain relaxation of the muscles of your lips.

9. Proceed to the nose, cheeks, ears and chin. Follow the same procedure. While you're doing the PMR, remember to inhale and exhale deeply. When all your muscles are relaxed, you will feel a sensation of numbness. Your muscles will feel heavy and "dead".

10. Other people prefer to start from the face and then down to the toes. You can choose whatever is more convenient for you.

B. Aerobic exercises

Aerobic exercises also help relax the mind and body. When your mind is relaxed, you can control your emotions properly. A healthy body yields a healthy mind. Aside from walking, here are other examples of outdoor aerobic exercises:

- o   Swimming

- o   Jogging

- o   Running

- o   Cycling

- o   Skiing

- o   Skating

For indoor aerobic exercises you can do:

- o   Treadmill

- o   Indoor walking/jogging

- o   Stationary bicycle

- o   Stairmaster

- o   Stair climbing

All these exercises are good for brain and body health. Take care of your brain and the brain will effectively help you manage your emotions.

C. Hypnosis

This can be one of the last options when the other methods won't work. Hypnosis can be dangerous to individuals with mental disorders because the procedure can aggravate the existing condition. So, if you decide to choose hypnosis, a competent and experienced hypnotist must perform the procedure.

D. Acupuncture

This is an alternative treatment for stress, pressure and frustrations. Acupuncture should only be done by a licensed acupuncturist. He will be inserting sterile needles into the reflex points or meridian points of the body to target vital body organs. Inserting needles at these specific points along the meridians is believed to re-balance the flow of life energy, or *qi*, which helps to cure ailments in the organs concerned.

The alternative methods you choose will depend upon what you're most comfortable with. Engaging in meditation, exercise and relaxation are essential to keeping a calm mind, so they must always be included in your strategies.

Chapter 6: Other Valuable Tips for Staying in Control

Uncontrolled emotions can wreak havoc in your life and bring about trouble. Knowing how to remain unaffected is a skill that you must learn as you go through life. That's why people say that you're already a mature person when you have gained emotional control. The following tips will help you achieve emotional control.

1. **Be an optimist.** Thinking positively will surely drive stress, pressure and frustrations away. You won't easily give in to negative stimuli because you will always believe that everything will eventually turn out well.

2. **Think of negative emotions as incidents that will soon pass.** Remembering that "all these will pass" will help you cope with all the negative emotions that you may encounter.

3. **Solicit moral support from family and friends.** When you feel downcast, you can ask

assistance from your family and trusted friends. Don't be afraid to seek help.

4. **Don't feel stressed, pressured or frustrated about past events.** Let bygones be bygones. There's no use crying over spilt milk. Instead, record what you have learned and move on from there.

5. **Don't feel stressed, pressured or frustrated about future events.** In the same manner stop worrying about future events that you don't have control over. This can make your life miserable. Pay attention only to people and events over which you have direct control, and then do something about it.

Letting the weather or the economy stress you is unwise and needlessly add to your frustrations. As long as it's not the end of the world, then trust that all will still be fine. Enjoy life more by eliminating things you should not worry about.

6. **Evaluate options carefully.** When working out plans for coping with stress and frustrations, choose the best alternative that will allow you to be calm and at peace. The

best alternative should be decided on after careful evaluation of the causes of your stress, pressure and frustrations. It should be convenient, effective and comfortable for you.

7. **You cannot control other people's feelings**. You can only control your own. So, make the best of it. Your level of maturity will reflect on your ability to manage your emotions.

8. **If you remain stressed, pressured and frustrated, consult a health specialist.** If the negative emotions persist even after implementing the steps presented here, consult a competent health specialist. An expert will help diagnose and identify other underlying conditions that are causing your stress and recommend appropriate remedies.

9. **Be patient.** Your habitual stressful and frustrated mode cannot be eliminated overnight. It may take several months or years before you can truly control your brain and stay calm during stressful situations. You will eventually reach your goal though. Just stay focused and keep going.

10. Learn to stop and pause. Life is short. Don't rush through it like an automaton. Take time to stop and enjoy your surroundings and the things around you. Pause to smell the roses and feel the wisp of air run across your face. Doing this will help you get rid of stress, pressure and frustrations.

These pointers will help you adapt, manage your emotions and cope with negative feelings. Being aware that "it's all in the mind" will help you cope with your feelings.

Conclusion

Managing your emotions takes persistence and determination. Understanding that you can control your emotions by using your brain is the first step in coping with negative emotions. Likewise, you can learn to control and use your emotions to your own advantage by practicing the steps presented in the previous chapters.

Knowing what you can control and what you cannot, can help reduce your stress and frustrations. Additionally, you can engage in a daily exercise regimen, perform meditation and relaxation activities to help you achieve a calm mind.

Now that you have the steps to gain control of your emotions, all you need is to persevere in following them properly and you're well on your way in being the master of your own feelings. Obviously, it's not as easy as it sounds. But if you're determined, you will certainly succeed. Remember, "It is all in the mind."

Finally, I'd like to thank you for purchasing this book! If you found it helpful, I'd greatly appreciate it if you'd take a moment to leave a review on Amazon. Thank you!